Nelson Comprehension

Pupil Book 6

OXFORD
UNIVERSITY PRESS

OXFORD
UNIVERSITY PRESS

Great Clarendon Street, Oxford, OX2 6DP, United Kingdom

Oxford University Press is a department of the University of Oxford.
It furthers the University's objective of excellence in research, scholarship,
and education by publishing worldwide. Oxford is a registered trade mark
of Oxford University Press in the UK and in certain other countries

Text © Wendy Wren 2016
Original illustrations except where stated © Oxford University Press 2016

The moral rights of the author have been asserted

First published by Nelson Thornes Ltd in 2009
This edition published by Oxford University Press in 2016

British Library Cataloguing in Publication Data
Data available

ISBN: 978-0-19-836823-6

3 5 7 9 10 8 6 4 2

Paper used in the production of this book is a natural, recyclable product made from wood
grown in sustainable forests. The manufacturing process conforms to the environmental
regulations of the country of origin.

Printed in China by Golden Cup

Acknowledgements
Cover illustration: Melanie Sharp

Illustrations: Paul Moran, Pete Smith, Studio Pulsar, Studio Bugs, Gary Joynes, Bob Moulder, Mark Draisey, Roger Penwill,
Russ Daff, Tony Forbes, Melanie Sharp, Mike Phillips, David Russell Illustration, p.12: Paul McCaffrey/Sylvie Poggio agency
and p.32: Abel Ippólito/Beehive Illustration.

Photographs: p.4(t): World History Archive / Alamy Stock Photo; p.4(b): North Wind Picture Archives / Alamy Stock Photo; p.6:
NASA; p.8: World History Archive / Alamy Stock Photo; p.16: Piti Tan / Shutterstock; p.28(t): Deejpilot / iStock; p.28(b): Neil
Mitchell / Shutterstock; p.30(t): Deejpilot / iStock; p.30(b): Carlos Arguelles / Shutterstock; p.40: Helen Hotson / 123RF; p.42: tom
pfeiffer / Alamy Stock Photo; p.44(t): Roman Krochuk / 123RF; p.44(b): Pictureguy / Shutterstock; p.56(t): iStock; p.56(m): strmko
/ iStock; p.56(b): strmko / iStock; p.58: National Library of Australia; p.60: Getty Images; p.62: Jesse Kraft / 123RF.

The author and publisher are grateful to the following for permission to reprint copyright material:

Clare Bevan: 'Coral Reef', copyright © Clare Bevan 2000, first published in *A Sea Creature Ate My Teacher* (Macmillan, 2000),
reprinted by permission of the author; Julie Holder: 'The Loner', copyright © Julie Holder 1982, first published in *A Fourth
Poetry Book* compiled by John Foster (OUP, 1982), reprinted by permission of the author; Patricia Leighton: 'Bullied', copyright
© Patricia Leighton 2002, first published in *The Works 2: poems on every subject and for every occasion* chosen by Michael Rosen
and Pie Corbett (Macmillan 2002), reprinted by permission of the author; Michael Morpurgo: extracts from *The Ghost of Grania
O'Mally* (Egmont, 1996), copyright © Michael Morpurgo 1996, and *Kensuke's Kingdom* (Egmont, 1999), copyright © Michael
Morpurgo 1999, reprinted by permission of David Higham Associates; extract from *Why The Whales Came* (Egmont, 2007),
copyright © Michael Morpurgo 1985, reprinted by permission of Egmont UK Ltd; Patrick Nobes: extract from *Frankenstein*
(Hutchinson Educational, 1984), copyright © Patrick Nobes, 1984, reprinted by permission of the author; Brian Patten: 'The
River's Story' from *Thawing Frozen Frogs* (Frances Lincoln, 2011), copyright © Brian Patten 1990, reprinted by permission of the
author c/o Rogers, Coleridge & White, 20 Powis Mews, London W11 1JN; Ian Serraillier: extract from *The Enchanted Island* (OUP,
1964), copyright © The Estate of Ian Serraillier, reprinted by permission of Jane Serraillier for the Estate of Ian Serraillier;
Joe Simpson: extract from *Touching the Void* (Jonathan Cape, 2004), reprinted by permission of The Random House Group Ltd;
Penny Stretton: extract from 'The Northern Lights Fantastic', *Daily Express*, 20 Dec 2008, reprinted by permission of Express
Newspapers.

Any third party use of this material, outside of this publication, is
prohibited. Interested parties should apply to the copyright holders
indicated in each case.

Although we have made every effort to trace and contact all copyright
holders before publication this has not been possible in all cases. If notified,
the publisher will rectify any errors or omissions at the earliest opportunity.

Oxford OWL
Discover eBooks, inspirational
resources, advice and support
www.oxfordowl.co.uk

Contents

UNIT 1

Emmeline Pankhurst

Emmeline Goulden was born in Manchester in 1858. Her father was a self-made man who had begun his working life as an office boy and risen to be a successful businessman. Emmeline grew up in a typical Victorian household where the father was master.

When Emmeline was fifteen, she was sent to Paris for her education. On her return, she married Richard Pankhurst who was a barrister. In the following years she had four children: Christabel, Sylvia, Frank and Ada. Emmeline had been a dutiful daughter; it now seemed as if she had settled into being a dutiful wife and mother.

Her husband, however, was not like her father. He had very different ideas about the role of women and encouraged Emmeline to see herself as his equal. Despite this, she soon realised that although she was an equal to her husband at home, outside she was just like other women – a second-class citizen. Women could not vote or become Members of Parliament so they had no power to change anything.

Emmeline, with a group of like-minded women, formed the WSPU (Women's Social and Political Union) and began to demand that women had the vote. The main political parties showed little interest in giving women the right to vote, despite massive demonstrations outside the Houses of Parliament. At this point, Emmeline decided there would be a change of tactics.

Members of the WSPU smashed windows, burned postboxes and set fire to unoccupied buildings. Some of the women were arrested and sent to jail. Emmeline was jailed for the first time in 1908. Women prisoners began hunger strikes and were brutally force-fed. When their health was in danger they were released, only to be re-arrested when their health improved.

This state of affairs continued until the beginning of the First World War. With the men away fighting, women turned their attention to keeping the country going: working in factories and on farms, driving ambulances, and generally doing all the work that their absent fathers, husbands and sons could not.

By the end of the war, it was generally accepted that women should have a right to vote. Women over the age of 30 were given the vote in 1918, but it was not until 1928, the year of Emmeline's death, that all women were given the vote on the same terms as men.

Teach

Understanding the text

1 Where and when was Emmeline born?

2 Where did she go for her education?

3 Whom did she marry?

4 What organisation did she form?

5 In what year could all women get the vote on the same terms as men?

Looking at language

6 Explain these phrases in your own words.

> **a** self-made man   **b** as his equal   **c** a second-class citizen
> **d** like-minded   **e** this state of affairs   **f** generally accepted

7 Explain the meaning of these words as they are used in the biography. Use a dictionary to help you.

> **a** barrister   **b** dutiful   **c** demonstrations
> **d** tactics   **e** unoccupied   **f** absent

Exploring the biography

8 Explain in your own words the phrase 'the father was master'.

9 In what way was Richard's attitude to women different from Emmeline's father's?

10 Why do you think that 'by the end of the war, it was generally accepted that women should have a right to vote'?

11 There are seven paragraphs in the biography. Briefly summarise each one.

12 How is the biography organised?

13 Why do you think the writer has included photographs?

Taking it further

▶ RB, Unit I, Extension

14 Present the information in the biography as a chart using these dates:
1858 / 1873 / 1908 / 1914 / 1918 / 1928

Teach

Neil Armstrong

Neil Alden Armstrong was born on 5 August 1930 in Wapakoneta, Ohio, in the United States. His father worked for the Ohio government and the family moved around the state, and lived in twenty different towns. He was fascinated by aeroplanes from a very early age and was determined to get his pilot's licence.

In 1947, after leaving Blume High School, Neil went to Purdue University to study aerospace engineering on a navy scholarship. In 1949, he was called up to serve in the navy, and eighteen months later he was a qualified naval aviator. He served as a navy pilot in the Korean War and flew 78 combat missions.

Back in America, he completed his science degree in 1955. He then worked for NASA (National Aeronautics and Space Administration) from 1955 to 1971. During the following years he worked as an engineer and test pilot. He flew 200 different types of aircraft, including jets, rockets, helicopters and gliders.

He applied, and was accepted, for astronaut training in 1962. Three years later, in 1965, he was the Command Pilot for *Gemini 8*. It was launched on 16 March 1966. The purpose of the mission was to dock with an unmanned craft, *Agena*, in space, and it was successfully accomplished.

On 23 December 1968, Armstrong was chosen as the Commander for *Apollo 11*, the manned mission to the moon. *Apollo 11* was to orbit the moon, and the lunar module, called *Eagle*, was to land on the surface. Along with Armstrong, Buzz Aldrin and Mike Collins made up the crew. Mike Collins would remain in *Apollo 11* while Armstrong and Aldrin landed on the moon in *Eagle*.

On 16 July 1969, *Apollo 11* was launched from the Kennedy Space Centre in Florida.

On 20 July, *Eagle* touched down on the moon's surface. Neil Armstrong was the first man to walk on the moon and, as he stepped out of the lunar module, he said, 'That's one small step for man, one giant leap for mankind.'

Armstrong and Aldrin spent a total of 21 hours and 36 minutes on the moon collecting samples of rock and dust. *Apollo 11* returned to Earth, 8 days, 3 hours and 18 minutes after take-off.

Armstrong worked at NASA until, in 1971, he became Professor of Aerospace Engineering at the University of Cincinnati. He has received many honours for his historic moon landing, including the Presidential Medal of Freedom and the NASA Distinguished Service Medal.
He died on 25 August 2012.

Talk

Understanding the text

1 Where was Neil Armstrong born?

2 When was he born?

3 What did he serve as in the Korean War?

4 When he completed his science degree, who did he work for?

5 What happened in:

    a 1962?   **b** 1966?   **c** 1969?

Looking at language

6 Explain the meaning of these phrases in your own words.

    a fascinated by   **b** pilot's licence   **c** called up
    d unmanned craft   **e** manned mission   **f** touched down

7 Explain the meaning of these words as they appear in the biography.
Use a dictionary to help you.

    a scholarship   **b** qualified   **c** aviator
    d accomplished   **e** mankind   **f** historic

Exploring the biography

8 What three pieces of evidence in the biography tell you that Armstrong was interested in flying?

9 Explain, in your own words, *Gemini 8*'s mission.

10 Why do you think the astronauts collected samples of moon 'rock and dust'?

11 Explain in your own words what you think Armstrong meant when he said 'That's one small step for man, one giant leap for mankind'.

12 There are eight paragraphs in the biography. Briefly summarise each one.

13 How is the biography organised?

Taking it further

▶ (RB, Unit I, Extension)

14 The other man who walked on the moon was Buzz Aldrin.
Research and write a short biography of Buzz Aldrin.

Talk

Louis Braille

Louis Braille was born in 1809, in the small town of Coupray, near Paris. His father made harnesses and other leather goods, and one of the tools he used was an awl. This is a short pointed stick used to punch holes into leather.

Louis liked to watch his father at work in his workshop. When he was three years old, he was playing with an awl when his hand slipped and he injured himself in the eye. At first, the wound did not seem too serious, but it became infected and within a few days Louis was blind in both eyes.

In the years that followed, he attended the local school. He was a very bright pupil, but learning was difficult because he could not read or write; he could only listen.

At the age of ten he was sent to the Royal Institute for Blind Youth in Paris. Here, Louis learned to read from books with raised letters, but the system was not very successful as it was difficult to tell the letters apart. Also, the books were bulky and expensive. The school only had fourteen of them. Louis read all of the fourteen books but it took a long time to work out the letters, then the words, and then the sentences. He was sure there must be a way to make 'reading' with his fingers quicker and easier.

One day, a soldier called Charles Barbier visited the school. He had invented a system called 'night writing' that allowed messages from officers to be read by soldiers in the dark. The system consisted of raised dots and dashes. The soldiers had to learn what the dots and dashes represented, then they could run their fingers over them to 'read' the message.

Louis tried the code and, although it was much better than the bulky books, it was still very slow. The dashes took up a lot of space so very little could be written on each page. Louis spent a great deal of time trying to improve the 'night writing'. He wanted to make it less complicated and to get more words on a page.

In the school holiday he worked on the problem. The solution came to him by handling the very tool that had made him blind. He could use a blunt awl to make a raised dot alphabet. It consisted of up to six dots, arranged in different positions, to represent the letters of the alphabet.

He published his first Braille book in 1829 and by 1837 had added symbols for music and maths. His system, surprisingly, was not greeted with great enthusiasm, and it took many years before it was universally accepted.

•	:	••	••	•.	::	::	:.	.•	.:	:	:	::
a	b	c	d	e	f	g	h	i	j	k	l	m
::	:.	::	::	:.	.:	::	:.	:.	.:	::	::	:.
n	o	p	q	r	s	t	u	v	w	x	y	z

Write

Understanding the text

1 Where was Louis Braille born?

2 When was he born?

3 What happened to Louis when he was three years old?

4 Where was he sent when he was ten years old?

5 What did he do in 1829?

Looking at language

6 Explain these phrases in your own words.

   a not very successful   **b** consisted of   **c** less complicated
   d not greeted with great enthusiasm   **e** universally accepted

7 Explain the meaning of these words as they are used in the biography.
   Use a dictionary to help you.

   a harnesses   **b** infected   **c** bulky   **d** symbols

Exploring the biography

8 In what ways do you think only being able to listen to your teacher, but not
   being able to read and make notes, would be difficult?

9 Explain in your own words, how 'night writing' worked.

10 According to Louis, what was wrong with 'night writing'?

11 What impression do you get of Louis Braille from what you have read?

12 There are eight paragraphs in the biography. Briefly summarise each one.

13 How is the biography organised?

Taking it further

▶ (RB, Unit I, Extension)

14 Using the illustration of the Braille alphabet, write your own name
   in Braille.

Write

UNIT 2

Frankenstein

It was on a dark, sad night in November that I came to the end of my work.
Most of what I had done had never been tried by anyone else before. It was
quite impossible to get a perfect result from this first attempt. I had aimed at
beauty, but the face of the creature I made was horrible. His skin was yellow,
and hardly hid the muscles and arteries under it. His eyes were dull and the
whites were almost the same colour as the yellow skin. The eyes were deep
in his head. True, his hair was black and long, and his teeth were very white.
But these touches of beauty only made the rest of his face appear more horrible.

His limbs were the right shape, but they were huge. One of the most difficult
parts of the work was joining together the very tiny nerves and veins. Nobody had
tried this before, and there were no scientific tools with which to do it. I had to work
to a larger scale than normal, and I decided to make my creature eight feet high.

I looked down at this ugly thing, and wondered whether all my hard work
had been worth it. I had driven myself on, and was ill as a result. Often I had
almost given up the work, when I failed to do some particularly difficult part
of it. But always I had started again. And here was the result of a year's work.

I felt certain that I could now bring my creation to life. The body was linked up
with the wires and switches that would make use of electrical power to give it life.

As I looked at the ugly creation, I almost decided to destroy it and forget the
whole idea. I wish I had. But I was not strong enough to turn away from the
dream of being the creator of a race of beings who would serve me as their
master. I wanted to use my great scientific powers to become a sort of god.

So I decided to carry on. A storm was building up over the city. I watched it and waited.
Suddenly at about one in the morning, the storm broke. Within moments my mast was
doing its work, and feeding down the power that I needed to put the spark of life into
my creation. I watched, and moved the controls of my machines. Would it all work?

For some time nothing happened, and I began to wonder whether all
my work had been in vain.

And then I saw the yellow eyes of the creature open. They moved from side
to side. Then its chest began to move up and down and I could hear the sound of
breathing. Soon the control board showed the steady beating of the heart. I fed
in more power through the limbs, and the arms and legs began to jerk into life.

The creature began to move, and slowly sat up. I realized that it was even
more horrible in life than it had been lying there with no life in it. My dream
had been one of beauty, and instead I had created
an ugly monster. My only wish was to escape from it,
and I had no other thought in my mind. I ran out of
the laboratory, and slammed the door behind me.
I was full of disgust at what I had done.

Adapted by Patrick Nobes from the novel by **Mary Shelley**

Understanding the text

1 When does this part of the story take place?

2 What did the creature look like?

3 Why has the narrator 'almost given up his work'?

4 How did the narrator bring the creature to life?

5 What did the narrator do when the creature 'slowly sat up'?

Looking at language

6 Explain these phrases in your own words.

    a had been worth it   **b** felt certain   **c** the storm broke
    d within moments   **e** in vain   **f** full of disgust

7 Explain the meaning of these words as they are used in the story. Use a dictionary to help you.

    a attempt   **b** arteries   **c** limbs
    d particularly   **e** creation   **f** power

Exploring the story

8 Find evidence in the story to suggest the narrator was a scientist.

9 Explain in your own words what the narrator's 'dream' was.

10 In what way had he succeeded?

11 In what way had he failed?

12 What impression do you get of the narrator?

13 We know how the narrator felt when the creature came to life. How do you think the creature felt?

Taking it further

RB, Unit 2, Extension

Teach

14 What do you think happens next? Write the next part of the story.

Theseus and the Minotaur

Minos, the ruler of Crete, had a huge army. He promised he would not attack the King of Athens, if the King sent him seven young men and seven young women to be fed to the terrible monster called the Minotaur. The King of Athens' son, Theseus, said he would go and kill the Minotaur.

When Theseus and the other young men and women arrived in Crete, they were treated very well. They were given the most delicious food. They took part in races and boxing matches.

Minos's daughter, Ariadne, got to know Theseus and was distraught to think of what was going to happen to him. She loved her father but thought what he was doing was very cruel. Going into the labyrinth meant automatic death. She had to think of a plan!

Soon it was time for the young people to be fed to the Minotaur. Ariadne secretly visited Theseus. 'The Minotaur lives in a labyrinth under the palace. No one has ever found a way out. The Minotaur catches and eats anyone who goes inside. You must make sure you are the first to go into the labyrinth,' she said.

'How will that help?' asked Theseus.

'Take this ball of string with you. Tie one end to the door and unroll it as you go. It will help you find your way out. I will wait at the door at midnight. If you are successful, I will show you a way out of the city,' she explained. 'You must take me with you. In the circumstances, I will not be safe here.' She looked around with fear in her eyes as if her father was watching her.

Early next morning, the guards came to take Theseus to the labyrinth. As soon as the door was closed behind him, he tied one end of the ball of string to it. He looked around at the gloomy passages. The labyrinth was the coldest and dampest place he had ever been in. He shivered. Would he ever escape from this horrible tomb?

He began to follow the winding passages, unrolling the ball of string as he went. Soon he could hear a terrifying noise. It was like the bellow of an angry animal, snorting and roaring. Theseus's mouth went dry and his hands became sweaty.

He followed the noise and came to a chamber in the middle of the labyrinth. Here, he had his first sight of the Minatour. It had a huge, human body but the head and neck of a bull! Theseus saw the bones of the Minotaur's victims scattered on the floor.

The Minotaur charged towards him. Theseus had no weapon, but his fist was a battering ram. He punched the creature in the heart and then leapt aside. Again and again the Minotaur charged. Again and again, Theseus struck him in the heart and leapt aside.

Soon the Minotaur began to grow weaker. Theseus leapt onto its back and grabbed its horns. He pulled with all his might until he heard a mighty crack. He had broken the Minotaur's neck. The creature fell to the ground – dead.

Theseus retraced his steps to the door, using the string Ariadne had given him. She was waiting there and together they escaped from Crete to safety.

Retold by **Wendy Wren**

Talk

Understanding the text

1 Where did Theseus live?

2 Who was Ariadne?

3 What was going to happen to Theseus?

4 What did Ariadne give to Theseus?

5 What did Theseus use as a weapon?

Looking at language

6 Explain these phrases in your own words.

    a automatic death   **b** in the circumstances   **c** horrible tomb

7 Explain the meaning of these words as they are used in the story.
Use a dictionary to help you.

    a delicious   **b** distraught   **c** labyrinth
    d gloomy   **e** victims   **f** retraced

Exploring the story

8 What impression do you get of Theseus?

9 What impression do you get of Ariadne?

10 How do you think Theseus felt when:
    a he was locked in the labyrinth?
    b he heard the noises the Minotaur made?

11 How do you think Ariadne felt as she waited outside?

12 What evidence tells you that other people had been killed in the labyrinth?

13 Explain in your own words how Theseus was able to defeat the Minotaur with no weapons.

Taking it further

▶ (RB, Unit 2, Extension)

14 Imagine you are Ariadne and write the story from her point of view.
Remember to describe what you see and hear, and how you are feeling.

Talk

Jurassic Park

John Hammond has recreated the world of dinosaurs on a remote island.
These dinosaurs are not models – they are the real thing! He keeps them behind
electric fences. He invites Dr Alan Grant to come and see them. John Hammond
sends his grandchildren, Tim and Lex, and Dr Grant on a tour of the island in electric
cars. Dr Grant and Ian are in one car, and Tim, Lex and Gennaro are in another.
Suddenly the power fails, just as they are outside the Tyrannosaurus paddock!

'Did you feel that?' Tim asked. At first Lex didn't know what he was talking about. But then she felt it, too. The car was shaking.

There were loud quaking sounds and it seemed as though the earth was moving – like something was taking giant footsteps.

Gennaro's eyes widened in fear. The sound got louder. The vibrations felt stronger. Whatever it was was coming closer. And then they all saw it. Tyrannosaurus rex. It was gripping the fence. Gennaro stared in horror. Oh no, he thought. The dinosaur should have felt an electric shock. The power must be out in the fences, too! But would it break through?

The T-rex swung its mighty head. Tim gasped. Its boxy head was bigger than Tim's whole body. And its body was bigger than a bus. The dinosaur waved its short, silly-looking arms in the air. Then it clawed the fence. The Tyrannosaurus was tearing it down!

All at once Gennaro bolted out of the car. He didn't say a word. He just ran, leaving Tim and Lex all alone. Lex began to scream. But Gennaro didn't stop. He raced towards a small building a short distance down the road. Moments later, he reached it and ran inside. But the building wasn't finished yet. Gennaro couldn't lock the wooden door behind him.

'What's he doing?' Ian asked Alan. They hadn't noticed the Tyrannosaurus yet.

Then they saw the fence come down. The Tyrannosaurus was free! It stood on the park road, eyeing the two cars.

'Don't move,' Alan whispered to Ian, 'It can't see us if we don't move.'

The T-rex bent down. It peered through the car window at Ian. Ian froze. He couldn't have moved if he'd wanted to.

Suddenly the first car lit up like a beacon. Lex had turned on a flashlight. The dinosaur raised its head. It was drawn to the light.

'I'm sorry, sorry, sorry,' Lex mumbled to Tim as the T-rex thudded closer.

It lifted its head high. Tim and Lex could see it through the sunroof.

Roar! The dinosaur opened its mouth wide, then roared again. It was so loud, the car windows rattled.

Then the T-rex struck.

The dinosaur lifted its powerful leg. Smash! It kicked the car. Windows shattered, and the car tilted on its side. The dinosaur lowered its head and butted the car off the road.

Inside, Tim and Lex tumbled about as the car rolled over. Now it was upside down. Tim twisted around to look out the window. They were right by the cliff.

The T-rex towered over the car. It put one leg on the frame and tore at the undercarriage of the car with its jaws. Biting at anything it could get a hold of, it ripped the rear axle free, tossed it aside, and bit a tyre. Lex and Tim were trapped. And the dinosaur was about to push them over the cliff!

Adapted by Gail Herman from the novel by **Michael Crichton**

Write

Understanding the text

1 What has John Hammond recreated?
2 Where are the characters at the beginning of the extract?
3 Why could the T-rex grip the fence?
4 What did Gennaro do when he saw the T-rex?
5 Why did Alan say, 'Don't move'?

Looking at language

6 Explain the meaning of these words as they are used in the story.
Use a dictionary to help you.

    a quaking   **b** vibrations   **c** bolted
    d eyeing   **e** beacon   **f** butted

Exploring the story

7 How does the author create a feeling of fear in the first three paragraphs?
8 What impression do you get of Gennaro?
9 How do you know that Dr Alan Grant knows something about dinosaurs?
10 Why do you think Lex turned on the flashlight?
11 What do you think Dr Alan Grant and Ian do when they
see what is happening to Tim and Lex?

Taking it further

▶ (RB, Unit 2, Extension)

12 Imagine you are Tim or Lex. Rewrite the extract
from your point of view.
Remember:
- you don't know what Alan and Ian are doing.
- you only know what is happening in
your car and what you can see
through the windows.
- include your thoughts
and feelings as
you tell the story.

Write

Text Messaging – Good or Bad?

Many adults are worried about the effect text messaging is having on the standard of written English of young people today. Others think that any form of communication between young people should be encouraged. So what are the advantages and disadvantages of text messaging?

Firstly, text messaging is a form of communication that young people are very enthusiastic about. Adults should not try to stop it just because they don't understand it and probably can't do it! They should realise that text messaging is spreading into the business world, so some adults see it as a very positive thing.

Another advantage of text messaging is that it is very fast. A text can be sent and replied to in a matter of seconds, almost like speaking face to face. There is no need to log on at a computer as is the case when sending an email.

Perhaps one of the most important advantages for young people is that text messaging is a very private form of communication. Unlike a conversation or telephone call that can be overheard, a text can be read just by the person it is sent to, unless he or she chooses to show it to others. The reply is equally private.

There are, however, serious disadvantages when it comes to the rules of text messaging creeping into written English. Parents and teachers have seen the symbols and abbreviations of text messaging in their children's school work.

Spelling is an obvious problem. It is a fact that some young children are convinced that text spelling is correct, for example that 'great' is always 'gr8', whether texting or writing. Vowels are usually missed out altogether.

Punctuation is another area of concern. As it doesn't exist in the rules of text messaging, it is fast disappearing from written work. In text messaging punctuation is only used to form symbols, for example, :) means 'I'm happy'.

Text messaging is also having an effect on children's vocabulary. Messages are written in a kind of shorthand so children express themselves in stock phrases and come to rely on a very limited vocabulary, no matter what the situation.

So what is to be done? Banning text messaging is unrealistic and would stop a very valuable form of communication. Allowing the rules of text messaging to go uncorrected in written work would seriously affect the standard of children's education. The answer is to teach children 'appropriate' language. Just as they understand that the way they speak to friends is different from the way they speak to their parents and teachers, so we should help them to appreciate the different rules of text messaging and standard English. Neither one is right; neither one is wrong. It is only when they are used in the wrong way that the problems occur.

Teach

Understanding the text

1 What is the article about?

2 According to the article, what are the advantages of text messaging?

3 What are the disadvantages?

4 Who are very enthusiastic about text messaging?

5 Who may try to stop it?

Looking at language

6 Explain these phrases in your own words.

a positive thing   b face to face   c fast disappearing
d stock phrases   e limited vocabulary

7 Explain the meaning of these words as they are used in the article.
Use a dictionary to help you.

a communication   b enthusiastic   c overheard   d abbreviations
e convinced   f concern   g shorthand   h unrealistic

Exploring the article

8 What do you think is the purpose of the first paragraph?

9 Who do you think is the intended audience?

10 What do you think the writer's attitude to text messaging is?

11 Explain in your own words the conclusion the writer comes to.

12 Do you think the conclusion is sensible or not? Explain your reasons.

13 What do you think about text messaging?

Taking it further

▶ RB, Unit 3, Extension

14 Present the information in the article in the form of a chart.

Teach

Animal Testing

When we are ill and visit the doctor or go into hospital, we expect that the drugs we are given or the operations we have to undergo to make us better are safe. Extensive research is done on these drugs and procedures in laboratories all over the world and, for some of this work, it is necessary to use animals.

Animal testing has been essential in making such procedures as heart, lung and kidney transplants, cataract operations and joint replacements viable. This means that humans can live longer and have a better quality of life. Reducing or banning animal testing would have serious consequences for the future of medical research and the benefits it brings to us.

Many people think that animal testing is not necessary. They claim that research can be done in other ways. This is not true. Wherever possible, scientists use other methods such as computer modelling and, as a result, the number of animals used in the last 30 years has halved. However, in many cases, these non-animal methods are not suitable. The only way for some medical advances to be made is through close study of how animals react to drugs and operations.

Scientists involved in animal testing do not do so lightly, and they are constantly striving to find alternative means to make drugs and medical procedures safe for humans. They follow a code known as the 'Three Rs':

- **R**eplacement   – to replace animal procedures with non-animal techniques wherever possible
- **R**eduction   – to minimise the number of animals used
- **R**efinement   – to improve the way experiments are carried out to make sure animals suffer as little as possible.

The use of animals in medical research is closely regulated. In 1986, The Animal Act was passed, and scientists have to prove that the cost of the research and the potential suffering of any animal involved are far out-weighed by the likely benefits to humans. A team of inspectors, who are vets or doctors, are employed by the government to ensure that all animal testing is done to these high standards.

That animal suffering occurs is not denied. But we have to ask ourselves a simple question. If we, or our loved ones, are faced with a life-threatening condition, do we not want medical researchers to have done everything possible to make the treatment safe and effective? Yes or no?

A survey by MORI found that 90 per cent of the public accepted the need for animal testing provided that:

- the research is for serious medical or life-saving purposes
- there is no alternative
- there is no unnecessary suffering.

So, 90 per cent of the public said 'Yes'.

Understanding the text

1 What is the article about?

2 What has happened in the last 30 years?

3 What are the 'Three Rs'?

4 When was the Animal Act passed?

5 What does it make scientists do?

Looking at language

6 Explain these phrases in your own words.

a extensive research	**b** quality of life	**c** serious consequences
d closely regulated	**e** out-weighed	**f** life-threatening condition

7 Explain the meaning of these words as they are used in the article. Use a dictionary to help you.

a undergo	**b** procedures	**c** viable	**d** striving
e minimise	**f** potential	**g** denied	**h** effective

Exploring the article

8 What is the purpose of the first paragraph?

9 Who do you think is the intended audience?

10 The article says that the scientists involved in animal testing 'do not do so lightly'. What does this mean?

11 Under what conditions must animals be tested for 90% of people to agree to it?

12 What do you think is the writer's attitude to animal testing?

13 Are you convinced by the writer's arguments? Why? Why not?

Taking it further

▶ RB, Unit 3, Extension

Talk

14 What arguments would you put forward to stop animal testing?

UFOs Do Not Exist!

Strange lights in the sky! People claiming to have been abducted by aliens! The *X Files* and *Independence Day* warning us to be prepared to fight the 'baddies' from distant planets to protect our world! Well, maybe.

Let's look at the facts. These so-called unidentified flying objects are usually seen by very ordinary people, at night, and in lonely rural areas. They are almost always 'sighted' by a person on his or her own and no physical evidence is left to prove their story.

When UFOs were first 'sighted' in the 1950s, believers were convinced that Earth was being visited by Martians, Venusians, or other inhabitants of our solar system. When American and Russian space probes visited these planets and found them unable to support life, the UFO enthusiasts changed their minds and said that the 'aliens' must be from other galaxies! Their technology is so advanced they can travel faster than the speed of light to come and have a look at us.

But for what purpose? Suppose we say UFOs do exist. Suppose that we accept there are technologically superior beings who travel millions, if not billions, of light years to pay us a visit and then go away again. It doesn't make any sense. Why don't they make contact with our world leaders if they come in peace? Why don't they use their superior technology to take over our planet if they are not so peaceful? Why do they buzz around the countryside, allowing their spaceships to be seen by relatively few people, and then disappear again?

People will argue that it is not just the lone individual on a back road in the dead of night who claims to have seen strange lights in the sky, and they are right. Let's take the recent example of the 'four large glowing lights in the sky' that were reported by dozens of people from all over Wiltshire. So many people saw them, surely this is the proof we have been waiting for? Well, no. SUFOR – the Swindon UFO Research group – had to admit there was a very ordinary explanation. Cirencester College was open to the public that evening and they put on a light show that used powerful space tracer lights straight up into the sky. The light show stopped at 9.30pm and, not surprisingly, the sighting of the alien visitors stopped at the same time!

And finally – in the USA alone, five million people have claimed that they have been abducted by aliens in the last 50 years. That's 2,470 visits from UFOs every day. I wonder why I haven't seen one.

Understanding the text

1 What is the article about?

2 When do UFO sightings usually happen?

3 Where do they usually happen?

4 When were UFOs first sighted?

5 In the fourth paragraph, what is the writer puzzled about?

Looking at language

6 Explain these phrases in your own words.

    a so-called   **b** physical evidence   **c** support life
    d changed their minds   **e** technologically superior

7 Explain the meaning of these words as they are used in the article.
Use a dictionary to help you.

    a abducted   **b** rural   **c** unidentified
    d Venusians   **e** enthusiasts   **f** galaxies

Exploring the article

8 What is the purpose of the first paragraph?

9 Who do you think is the intended audience?

10 In your own words, explain what happened at Cirencester College.

11 The writer repeats that most UFO 'sightings' are reported by people who are alone. What is the writer implying?

12 What do you think is the writer's attitude to UFOs?

13 Does the writer want the final paragraph to be taken seriously or not? Give reasons for your answer.

14 Are you convinced by the writer's arguments? Why? Why not?

Taking it further

▶ RB, Unit 3, Extension

Write

15 What arguments would you put forward to say that UFOs do exist?

The Loner

He leans against the playground wall,
Smacks his hands against the bricks
And other boredom-beating tricks,
Traces patterns with his feet,
Scuffs to make the tarmac squeak,
Back against the wall he stays –
And never plays.

The playground's quick with life,
The beat is strong.
Though sharp as a knife
Strife doesn't last long.
There is shouting, laughter, song,
And a place at the wall
For who won't belong.

We pass him running, skipping, walking,
In slow huddled groups, low talking.
Each in our familiar clique
We pass him by and never speak,
His loneness is his shell and shield
And neither he nor we will yield.

He wasn't there at the wall today,
Someone said he'd moved away
To another school and place
And on the wall where he used to lean
Someone had chalked
'Watch this space.'

Julie Holder

Understanding the text

1 When and where is the poem set?

2 What does the 'loner' do?

3 What noises can be heard?

4 What do the other children do?

5 What do the children never do?

Looking at language

6 The playground is described as 'quick with life'. Explain this phrase in your own words.

7 Explain the meaning of these words as they are used in the poem. Use a dictionary to help you.

    a scuffs   **b** strife   **c** huddled
    d clique   **e** yield

Exploring the poem

8 Explain in your own words what you understand by the word 'loner'.

9 How do you know the loner is bored?

10 What does the poet mean when she writes, 'And a place at the wall / For who won't belong'?

11 Whose fault is it, do you think, that the loner doesn't play with the others?

12 How do you think:
    a the loner feels about the other children?
    b the other children feel about the loner?

13 What do you think the poet means by the last three lines of the poem?

Taking it further

▶ RB, Unit 4, Extension

14 In groups, learn and recite the poem. Use different people to say different verses.

Teach

Bullied

Bullies get you.
I don't know how but they do.
They seem to have some
secret inborn radar
tuned in to loners,
quiet ones,
different ones.

  You don't have to
  do anything, say anything.
  Seems you just have to be you.

Grown-ups think they know.
Bullies? Just cowards, they say,
unsure of themselves,
needing to act big.
But it's hard to believe
when jeering faces
zoom up to yours.

When they're hassling you,
calling you names,
leading the chanting,
the whispering,
urging the others on,
a relentless horde
of nagging, pecking birds.

Then there's the 'in-betweens',
the waiting, the not knowing,
just sure that
sooner or later
it's going to come.
The worst times;
the thinking times.

  Don't ask me the answer.
  I don't know but –
  I'm getting there.

Keep my eyes skinned,
find a crowd to vanish into
before *they see me*.
Cornered, I know I can't look them
in the eye – but I've learned
not to look at the floor,
to try and walk tall.

Mostly I've learned
to talk in my head,
tell myself
it's not me, I'm all right –
they're the idiots, the misfits.
Eventually
it begins to sink in.

I'm getting tougher inside.
It's working.
Just don't give in.

Try anything, anything.
But don't *let* them win.

Patricia Leighton

Talk

Understanding the text

1 According to the poem, whom do bullies pick on?

2 What does the poet say is the 'worst' time?

3 What is the poet learning to do to avoid being picked on?

4 What is she determined she must not do?

Looking at language

5 Explain these phrases in your own words.

    a eyes skinned   **b** walk tall   **c** sink in

6 Explain the meaning of these words as they are used in the poem.
Use a dictionary to help you.

    a radar   **b** unsure   **c** jeering
    d hassling   **e** relentless   **f** misfits

Exploring the poem

7 Explain in your own words what 'grown-ups' say about bullies.

8 In the fourth verse, what does the poet compare bullies to?
Explain why you think this is, or is not, a good comparison.

9 Why do you think the poet has learned 'not to look at the floor'?

10 Why do you think it is important that the poet believes 'it's not me,
I'm all right'?

Taking it further

▶ RB, Unit 4, Extension

11 **a** Why do you think people bully other people?
    b What advice would you give to someone who is being bullied?

Talk

The New Boy

The door swung inward. I stood and breathed
The new-school atmosphere:
The smell of polish and disinfectant,
And the flavour of my own fear.

I followed into the cloakroom; the walls
Rang to the shattering noise
Of boys who barged and boys who banged;
Boys and still more boys!

A boot flew by. Its angry owner
Pursued with force and yell;
Somewhere a man snapped orders;
   somewhere
There clanged a bell.

And there I hung with my new schoolmates
They pushing and shoving me; I
Unknown, unwanted, pinned to the wall;
On the verge of ready-to-cry.

Then, from the doorway, a boy called out:
'Hey, you over there! You're new!
Don't just stand there propping the wall up
I'll look after you!'

I turned; I timidly raised my eyes;
He stood and grinned meanwhile;
And my fear died, and my lips answered
Smile for his smile.

He showed me the basins, the rows of pegs
He hung my cap at the end;
He led me away to my new classroom …
And now that boy's my friend.

John Walsh

Write

Understanding the text

1 What is the setting for the poem?

2 What smells does the poet notice?

3 How do you know it is not quiet in the cloakroom?

4 When the poet was 'pinned to the wall', what was he about to do?

5 When did the poet's 'fear' die?

Looking at language

6 Explain these phrases in your own words.

> **a** snapped orders   **b** on the verge   **c** propping up

7 Explain the meaning of these words as they are used in the poem. Use a dictionary to help you.

> **a** atmosphere   **b** shattering   **c** barged
> **d** pursued   **e** clanged   **f** timidly

Exploring the poem

8 Find evidence that tells you how the boy was feeling at the beginning of the poem.

9 Find evidence that tells you how he was feeling at the end of the poem.

10 What impression is the poet trying to create with the words 'barged', 'banged' and 'pushing and shoving'?

11 Who do you think the man was who 'snapped orders'?

12 Do you think the boys were deliberately unkind to the poet? Why? Why not?

13 There were 'boys and still more boys' in the school. Why do you think it took only one boy being kind to the poet to make him feel better?

Taking it further

▶ RB, Unit 4, Extension

14 Imagine you had to move to a new school. Write about what you would look forward to and what you would be worried about.

Write

UNIT 5

The Tower of London

History of the Tower of London

William the Conqueror (1028–1087) built the Tower of London for the purpose of protecting the city. Tradition has it that it was started in 1078 and took 20 years to complete. The White Tower was the first stone keep to be built in Britain and is the only part left of the original building. Large quantities of stone were transported to the site to build the huge walls that extended 32.5 metres east / west, 36 metres north / south, and were 27.5 metres high. Over the centuries, the buildings on the site have been extended and now, including the moat, cover 18 acres.

In the reign of Henry III (1216–1272) the Tower was extended and enclosed by a new curtain wall. Edward I (ruled 1272–1307) continued improving the castle's defences by having two curtain walls, one inside the other. The inner wall was higher so the outer wall could be defended from it.

Throughout its history, the Tower of London has been fortress, palace and prison; the home of the Royal Mint and the Royal Observatory; housed a large arsenal of small arms and the Crown Jewels. From the 13th century onwards it was also the home of the Royal Menagerie that evolved into London Zoo.

Up until as late as the 17th century, control of the Tower of London was essential to control of London itself. The Tower was a stronghold from which London could be defended, but it was also a refuge for when the monarch was in danger. Safe within its walls, a monarch could organise his supporters or come to some agreement with the enemy – an enemy that was often the people of London, who were less than pleased with their monarch's actions.

The Tower of London became one of many royal houses. In many reigns it was hardly used at all, but almost every monarch stayed there before his or her coronation. After spending the night at the Tower, the monarch-to-be would ride in a great procession through the streets of London to Westminster Abbey to be crowned.

This procession was to please the people of London whose support was so important to a successful reign. The last of these processions from the Tower to the Abbey was made by Charles II in 1661.

Although no monarch has actually lived in the Tower of London for over 400 years, it still has the title of a royal palace.

Teach

Understanding the text

1 For what purpose was the Tower of London built?

2 What is 27.5 metres high?

3 How many acres does the site cover?

4 When did almost every monarch stay in the Tower of London?

5 Where are the kings and queens of England crowned?

Looking at language

6 These are all parts of the Tower of London. Explain what they are.
Use a dictionary to help you.

   a keep   **b** moat   **c** curtain wall   **d** arsenal

7 Explain the meaning of these words as they are used in the passage.
Use a dictionary to help you.

   a tradition   **b** original   **c** transported   **d** fortress
   e menagerie   **f** essential   **g** refuge   **h** coronation

Exploring the passage

8 Explain in your own words what you understand by 'Tradition has it that it was started in 1078'.

9 What do you think was the purpose of:
   a the Royal Mint?   **b** the Royal Observatory?

10 Why do you think the monarch had to please the people of London?

11 How has the writer ordered the information in the passage?

12 Do you think the photographs help the reader to understand the text? Why? Why not?

13 This is the introduction to a book about the Tower of London.
Do you think it is useful or not? Explain your reasons.

Taking it further

▶ RB, Unit 5, Extension

14 Create a table of information about the Tower of London by summarising the content of each paragraph.

Teach

A GUIDE TO

THE
TOWER OF
LONDON

One of Britain's most popular tourist attractions with several million visitors each year. This is a guide to the most popular parts of the Tower that should not be missed.

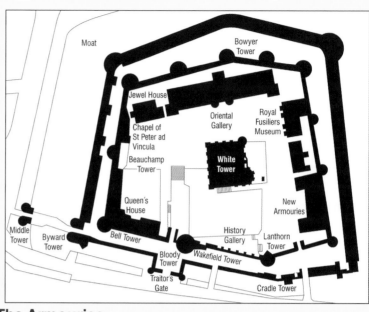

The Armouries

Housed in the White Tower, armour and weapons from the Middle Ages onward are displayed in the Armouries. The earliest examples are of chain mail for the body and legs. A helmet was worn and extra protection given by a shield carried on the left arm. Weapons were the lance and the sword and, to a lesser degree, the mace and the axe. As well as weapons and armour used for sport, tournaments and combat, one can also see an example of an execution block and axe. Oriental weapons are on display in the New Armouries to the east of the White Tower.

Traitor's Gate

Traitor's Gate is situated below St Thomas's Tower. It was originally a main entrance via the Thames. In later years it was used to bring prisoners to the Tower after they had been tried and convicted at Westminster. Such famous prisoners as Anne Boleyn, Sir Thomas More and Thomas Cromwell passed through these gates on the way to imprisonment or execution.

The Jewel House

Most of the jewels on display date from the 17th century as many of the earlier ones were melted down by Oliver Cromwell. The oldest crown to be seen was made for the coronation of Charles II. Other items, such as Queen Victoria's Imperial State Crown, sceptre, orbs and swords, can also be seen in the Jewel House.

The Wakefield Tower

Probably named after William de Wakefield, a senior court official in the reign of Edward III, it is most famous for being the scene of Anne Boleyn's trial. The second wife of Henry VIII failed to produce a male heir. Charges of treason were brought against her and she was executed in 1536.

The Bloody Tower

Formerly known as the Garden Tower, it was given its gruesome name because of the deaths of 'the Princes in the Tower'. Edward V (12) and his brother, the Duke of York (10), are thought to have been murdered by the Duke of Gloucester on his way to becoming King Richard III.

Talk

Understanding the text

1 Name two of the weapons that can be seen in the Armouries.

2 What was Traitor's Gate used for:
   a originally?   **b** in later years?

3 Who wore the Imperial State Crown at her coronation?

4 What is the Wakefield Tower most famous for?

5 Where were the Princes thought to have been murdered?

Looking at language

6 Explain these phrases in your own words.

> **a** tourist attraction   **b** to a lesser degree   **c** execution block
>
> **d** melted down   **e** male heir   **f** formally known as

7 Explain the meaning of these words as they are used in the guide.
   Use a dictionary to help you.

> **a** mace   **b** combat   **c** convicted   **d** sceptre
>
> **e** orbs   **f** treason   **g** executed   **h** gruesome

Exploring the guide

8 How do you think the writer of the guide worked out which are the 'most popular' parts of the Tower for visitors?

9 Why do you think 'Traitor's Gate' is so called?

10 Do you think Charles II ruled England before or after Oliver Cromwell? Explain your reasons.

11 Why do you think the Duke of Gloucester may have murdered the two princes?

12 Why do you think the writer has included a plan of the Tower of London?

13 What two parts of the Tower of London are we sure Anne Boleyn visited?

Taking it further

▶ (RB, Unit 5, Extension)

14 Using the plan of the Tower, work out a circular route so that the visitor sees everything in the guide.

Talk

Animals in the Tower

For 600 years, the Tower of London was home to a wide variety of exotic animals.

The first animals to come to the Tower were gifts. It is said that in 1235, Emperor Frederick II gave the English King Henry III three leopards. We now think that these animals were lions and we can still see them today on the England team's football shirts!

In 1252, a white polar bear arrived, given as a gift by the King of Norway, and in 1255, an African elephant came from the King of France.

As the years rolled by, wolves, eagles, hyenas, owls, ostriches, monkeys, baboons, panthers and alligators were residents of the Tower. Many didn't survive long in their cramped conditions, but some did a lot of damage before they died.

One of the big cats would seize umbrellas, parasols and hats from visitors and tear them to pieces. A group of monkeys attacked a boy and tore off his leg. A woman called Mary Jenkinson, not realising just how dangerous it could be, tried to stroke a lion. Her arm was badly mauled and she died from the amputation.

By the 1830s the animals had gone from the Tower. They were dangerous and expensive to keep, so some went to the new zoo in Regent's Park, while others went in a travelling show all the way to America.

The animals that can still be seen at the Tower are the ravens. There is a legend that says if the ravens ever leave the Tower of London then 'the kingdom will fall'. As a result, the ravens have always been looked after very well by the Raven Master. There must always be six of them, and a seventh is kept as a spare. They eat 170g of raw meat every day, biscuits, and egg once a week. Some do go missing, and some are 'sacked'. Raven George was dismissed for eating television aerials!

Write

Understanding the article

1 What animals came to the Tower in 1235?

2 When did the polar bear arrive?

3 What happened to Mary Jenkinson?

4 In the 1830s, where did the animals from the Tower end up?

5 What do the ravens eat?

Looking at language

6 Explain these phrases in your own words.

    a it is said that   **b** as the years rolled by   **c** as a result

7 Explain the meaning of these words as they are used in the article. Use a dictionary to help you.

    a residents   **b** survive   **c** seize
    d parasols   **e** mauled   **f** amputation

Exploring the article

8 What do you understand by the term 'exotic animals'?

9 In what way can we still see the lions on 'the England team's football shirts'?

10 How can you tell that the animals were not looked after very well?

11 What do you think 'the kingdom will fall' means?

12 Why do you think a seventh raven is 'kept as a spare'?

Taking it further

▶ RB, Unit 5, Extension

13 Have the three texts about the Tower of London made you want to visit it or not?
Explain your reasons.

Write

UNIT 6

Why the Whales Came

'As long as we keep Scilly Rock astern of us we can pull home easily enough,' Daniel said softly.

'But how are we going to do that if we can't see it?' I whispered, taking the oar he was handing me. 'I can't see it anymore.'

'We can hear it though, can't we?' he said. 'Listen.' And certainly I could hear the surge of the sea seething around Scilly Rock as it always did even on the calmest of days. 'Hear it?' he said. 'Just keep that sound astern of us and we'll be able to feel our way home. Gweal must be dead ahead from here. There's no swell to speak of, so we won't go on the rocks. All we have to do is to hug the coast all the way round and that'll bring us nicely into Popplestones.'

And so we began to row, only a few strokes at a time, stopping to listen for the sea around Scilly Rock. It was not long though before I began to think that Gweal was not at all where it should have been. We had already been rowing quite long enough and hard enough to have reached it by now. Then I thought that, perhaps the current must have dragged us off course, that we must be somewhere between Samson and Bryher, that I could still hear Scilly Rock somewhere astern of us and distant, but Daniel was no longer even sure of that. We pulled until our arms could pull no longer, but still no land loomed up out of the fog as we expected. Within half an hour we had to admit to each other that we were quite lost. We sat over our oars and drifted, straining our ears for the wash of the sea against the rocks, anything to give us some idea of where we were. The fog though seemed to obscure and shroud the sounds of the sea just as it was hiding the islands that we knew lay all around us. Even the piping of invisible oystercatchers was dulled and deadened as the dark came down through the fog and settled around us.

Strange as it may seem, the darkness came as a kind of comfort to us, for at least it was the kind of blindness we were accustomed to. Even Daniel who was never fond of the dark seemed relieved at the onset of night. We searched now for some crack in the blackness about us, a glimmer of a light from the shore that would guide us safely home. We sat beside each other huddled together and silent, the damp jibsail wrapped around us to keep out the cold, peering constantly into the impenetrable night and listening, always listening for the hiss of surf on the shingle or the distant muted charge of the waves against the cliffs.

Often during that long, long night our hopes were raised by the whisper of waves on some far shore, and we would row frantically towards it for a few minutes and then sit silent and listen again, only to discover it had been nothing but wishful thinking, a trick of the mind. Either it was that or we had simply been rowing the wrong way – we could never be sure which. In this dense darkness all sense of direction, time and space seemed to be distorted. Each time our hopes were raised only to be dashed, and each time the disappointment was all the more cruel and all the more lasting.

The cold had numbed my feet up to my knees and my hands could no longer feel the oar I was pulling. I wanted so much just to go to sleep, to give up and go to sleep. But Daniel would not let me.

Michael Morpurgo

Teach

Understanding the text

1 What is the setting for this part of the story?

2 How many characters are there?

3 What did Daniel say they could use to find their way home?

4 How did the characters try to keep warm?

5 How was the narrator feeling at the end of the extract?

Looking at language

6 Explain these phrases in your own words.

> **a** dead ahead   **b** hug the coast   **c** off course   **d** wishful thinking

7 Explain the meaning of these words as they are used in the story.
Use a dictionary to help you.

> **a** astern   **b** seething   **c** swell
> **d** loomed   **e** obscure   **f** onset
> **g** impenetrable   **h** muted   **i** distorted

Exploring the story

8 Why couldn't the characters see Scilly Rock?

9 Why do you think they only rowed 'a few strokes at a time'?

10 Explain in your own words why the narrator says, 'the darkness came as a kind of comfort to us'.

11 What does the narrator mean when she says, 'the whisper of waves on some far shore ... had been nothing but wishful thinking'?

12 Why do you think Daniel would not let the narrator go to sleep?

13 When you read this extract, how do you think the writer wants you to feel?

Taking it further

▶ (RB, Unit 6, Extension)

Teach

14 Write what you think happens next in the story.

Lost at Sea

Jessie Parsons lives on Clare Island. Her American cousin, Jack, comes to stay with her for the summer. Jessie's father takes them fishing but has to return home when his rod breaks, leaving the children on the rocks. Then disaster strikes!

That was the moment the fish caught on and Jack shouted, 'I've got one! I've got one!' He braced his legs and began to reel in furiously. Then he slipped. His legs went from under him and he was sliding past her towards the edge.

Instinctively, Jessie reached out for him. For a fleeting moment she had hold of his jeans, just long enough for Jack to cling on to a rock and stop his slide. But then Jessie herself was slipping, rolling over and over and over, trying to find something to clutch at, anything. But there was nothing, no way she could stop herself. She caught a glimpse of Jack throwing himself full-stretch on the rock to save her. Then she was over the edge and falling through the air. The sea smothered her before she could scream. The water came into her mouth and into her ears and she was sinking deeper and deeper and could do nothing about it.

She looked up. There was light up above her, light she knew she had to reach if she was to live, but her legs wouldn't kick and her flailing arms seemed incapable of helping her. She had often thought about how drowning would be, when she was out in her father's boat or crossing over from the mainland on the ferry. And now she was drowning. This was how it was. Her eyes were stinging, so she closed them. She closed her mouth too, so she wouldn't swallow any more seawater. But she had to breathe – she couldn't help herself. She gasped and the seawater came in again and she began to choke.

Then something was holding her down. She fought, but the grip tightened about her waist and would not let go. Her head broke water, and suddenly there was air, wonderful air to breathe. She was spluttering and coughing. Someone was shouting at her. It was Jack and he was holding her. 'It's me! It's me! Hang on, just hang on to me. You'll be OK.' His face was near hers. 'Can you swim?' She shook her head. 'Just try to keep your mouth closed. Someone'll see us. We'll be OK. We'll be fine.'

Jessie looked beyond him. The shore was already a long way off and they were being carried away from it all the time. She looked the other way. Whenever they came up to the top of a wave she could see the bank of mist rolling over the sea towards them. One more wave and the mist would swallow them and then no one would ever see them.

'We've got to keep floating,' Jack cried. 'Just hang on.' The cold had numbed her legs already and she knew her arms couldn't hold on much longer. And then the mist came over their heads and shrouded them completely. Jack was crying out for help, screaming. She tried herself, but could only manage a whimper.

It was hopeless.

The Ghost of Grania O'Malley, **Michael Morpurgo**

Understanding the text

1 What are the two settings for this extract?

2 What caused Jack to slip?

3 What was Jessie trying to do when she slipped?

4 What happened before she could scream?

5 What did Jack say they had to keep doing?

Looking at language

6 Explain these phrases in your own words.

> **a** braced his legs   **b** fleeting moment   **c** caught a glimpse of
> **d** hang on   **e** it was hopeless

7 Explain the meanings of these words as they are used in the story.
   Use a dictionary to help you.

> **a** furiously   **b** instinctively   **c** flailing
> **d** numbed   **e** shrouded   **f** whimper

Exploring the story

8 What do you think was going through Jessie's mind as she was 'flailing'?

9 Why do you think she 'fought' when Jack was trying to rescue her?

10 Do you think Jack believed what he was saying when he said, 'We'll be fine'?
    Explain your reasons.

11 Explain in your own words why Jessie did not believe him.

12 How do you think Jack felt when:
    a he saw Jessie going into the water?
    b he dived in to save her?
    c he was 'crying out for help'?

Taking it further

▶ (RB, Unit 6, Extension)

13 What do you think Jack and Jessie can do to save themselves?

Talk

Alone in the Ocean

Michael's parents are both made redundant. His father decides to buy a boat called the Peggy Sue. *So Michael, his mum and dad, and their dog Stella, set off to sail round the world. One night his parents are sleeping and Michael is in charge of the boat. Stella is barking and she hasn't got her safety harness on …*

… So I left the wheel and went forward to bring her back. I took the ball with me to sweeten her in, to tempt her away from the bow of the boat.

I crouched down. 'Come on, Stella,' I said, rolling the ball from hand to hand. 'Come and get the ball.' I felt the boat turn a little in the wind, and I knew then I shouldn't have left the wheel. The ball rolled away from me quite suddenly. I lunged after it, but it was gone over the side before I could grab it. I lay there on the deck watching it bob away into the darkness. I was furious with myself for being so silly.

I was still cursing myself when I thought I heard the sound of singing. Someone was singing out there in the darkness. I called but no one replied. So that was what Stella had been barking at.

I looked again for my ball, but by now it had disappeared. That ball had been very precious to me, precious to all of us. I knew I had just lost a great deal more than a football.

I was angry with Stella. The whole thing had been her fault. She was still barking. I couldn't hear the singing anymore. I called her again, whistled her in. She wouldn't come. I got to my feet and went forward. I took her by the collar and pulled. She would not be moved. I couldn't drag her all the way back, so I bent down to pick her up. She was still reluctant. Then I had her in my arms, but she was struggling.

I heard the wind above me in the sail. I remember thinking: this is silly, you haven't got your safety harness on, you haven't got your lifejacket on, you shouldn't be doing this. Then the boat veered violently and I was thrown sideways. With my arms full I had no time to grab the guard rail. We were in the cold of the sea before I could even open my mouth to scream.

The terrors came fast, one upon another. The lights of the *Peggy Sue* went away in the dark of the night, leaving me alone in the ocean, alone with the certainty that they were already too far away, that my cries for help could not possibly be heard. I thought then of sharks cruising the black water beneath me – scenting me, already searching me out, homing in on me – and I knew there could be no hope. I would be eaten alive. Either that or I would drown slowly. Nothing could save me.

Kensuke's Kingdom, **Michael Morpurgo**

Write

Understanding the text

1 What is the setting for the extract?

2 Why did Michael think Stella was barking?

3 Why did he pick up the dog?

4 Why did he think he was being silly?

5 What two things frightened Michael when he was in the water?

Looking at language

6 Explain these phrases in your own words.

   a made redundant   **b** sweeten her   **c** no hope

7 Explain the meaning of these words as they are used in the story.
Use a dictionary to help you.

   a lunged   **b** precious   **c** reluctant   **d** veered   **e** cruising

Exploring the story

8 In your own words, explain why Michael 'shouldn't have left the wheel'.

9 Why do you think the ball was 'very precious' to him?

10 What safety equipment was:

   a the dog without?   **b** Michael without?

11 How do you think Michael felt when he was plunged into 'the cold of the sea'?

12 How do you think Michael gets to safety?

Taking it further

RB, Unit 6, Extension

13 Read the three extracts by Michael Morpurgo again.
Which one would persuade you to find and read the whole book?

Write

The Daily News

21st January

The Beast of Bodmin Moor

By Henry Harris

For 30 years or more, an unidentified 'Beast' has been terrorising the inhabitants and killing livestock in Cornwall, south-west England. Some think the mysterious creature is a puma; others that it is a leopard or a panther.

It was allegedly first spotted in 1983 and there have been at least 60 reported sightings ever since.

Mr Jones, a local farmer, claims that it has 'huge yellow eyes and a high-pitched scream.' His neighbour, Mrs Gerrans, came face to face with it. 'It jumped over that fence and went into that wood. I reckon it was about 3 feet long with brown fur.'

So, has there been any hard evidence? A skull with large fangs was found in the River Fowey. The skull measured about 10cm long by 18cm wide. The Natural History Museum in London was consulted and an expert concluded that this was the skull of a young male leopard that had not died in Britain. It turned out to be part of an imported leopard-skin rug!

What has the government done about the reported sightings? In 1995, Charlie Wilson, a wildlife biologist from the Agriculture Ministry was sent to investigate. He said, 'We're not doubting the honesty and sincerity of the people, but if we are going to submit a report and do something, we need to see hard evidence.'

Some six months and many thousands of pounds later, he wrote a report that claimed there was no 'verifiable evidence' of

any large cats roaming the moor. Experts examined photos and video evidence and came to the conclusion that the 'beast' was a black cat about 30cm in height.

Local people are not convinced by the report, and the sightings continue. Henry Warren was taking pictures of his new house when he 'saw something run across the field' in front of his lens. 'It was absolutely massive and was hopping up and down like a large cat. There was no way it was a dog or a fox.'

So, if big cats roam Bodmin Moor, where do local people think they have come from? Some believe they could have escaped from a zoo or private collection and have not been reported because they were imported illegally. Others believe it is a species of wildcat that became extinct in Britain more than 100 years ago.

Whatever you believe, should you find yourself alone on Bodmin Moor as night is falling, you can be forgiven for looking around to make sure the 'Beast' isn't stalking you!

Teach

Understanding the text

1 Where has the 'Beast' been sighted?

2 When was it first spotted?

3 Who came face to face with it?

4 What was found in the River Fowey?

5 Who did the government send to investigate it?

Looking at language

6 Explain these phrases in your own words.

  a face to face   **b** hard evidence   **c** verifiable evidence

7 Explain the meaning of these words as they are used in the article. Use a dictionary to help you.

  a terrorising   **b** allegedly   **c** consulted   **d** imported
  e investigate   **f** massive   **g** illegally   **h** species

Exploring the article

8 Why do you think the report includes what people in the area say about the 'Beast'?

9 Why do you think an expert from the Natural History Museum was consulted?

10 Why do you think 'local people are not convinced' by the report?

11 Give an example from the article of:
   a a fact.   **b** an opinion.

12 What do you think the reporter thinks of the Beast of Bodmin Moor?

Taking it further

▶ (RB, Unit 7, Extension)

13 Are you convinced by any of the explanations? Write a paragraph to explain why or why not.

Teach

ISLANDS OF Fire

Tongatapu, in the Pacific Ocean to the east of Australia, lies in the island group known as Tonga. On Monday 16 March 2009, about six miles from Tongatapu, an underwater volcano began erupting. By Wednesday 18 March, so much lava had been ejected that it had formed a new island. On Thursday 19 March, a huge earthquake measuring 7.9 on the Richter scale occurred.

An eruption of Anak Krakatau.

▲ Perboewatan

Anak Krakatau

Island before ——— Danan
26 August 1883

▲ Rakata

Krakatoa Island

0   3 km

Krakatoa as it was before ... and after the explosion.

Fear of imminent danger to the surrounding islands prompted the Tsunami Warning Centre to issue a serious alert. Luckily, no damage or loss of life was reported.

The new island is made from pumice that is formed when lava cools rapidly. It is very light and can float. Experts agree that the island will last several months or possibly a few years but, in time, it will be eroded by the sea. A spokesman for the team of scientists on their way to the new island said that they were going to observe the eruption and, when things had quietened down, measure the island.

As well as volcanic eruptions creating islands, they can also make islands virtually disappear. One of the most famous examples is Krakatoa off the southwest coast of Indonesia.

In 1883, Krakatoa covered an area of 23 square kilometres to a height of 450 metres above sea level. On 20 May, there were reports of a plume of smoke rising 10 kilometres above the island. Minor eruptions continued from May to August, and on 27 August 1883, a series of huge volcanic eruptions occurred, resulting in most of the island being submerged 250 metres below sea level.

Reports at the time say that the final explosion was heard 4,500 kilometres away and caused 40-metre-high tsunamis that completely submerged many small islands. The major islands of Java and Sumatra were devastated: whole towns and villages were destroyed and nearly all vegetation was stripped away.

Ships suffered a similar fate, with most being destroyed in the enormous waves. The *Berouw*, a steamship in the area, was carried 10 metres above sea level and deposited a mile inland.

It has been estimated that over 36,000 people lost their lives, either from the volcanic eruption that rained down ash and produced lava flows that reached up to 700°C, or from the ensuing tsunamis. As far away as the east coast of Africa, rafts of pumice were washed up, sometimes with a grizzly cargo of human remains.

And Krakatoa has not finished yet. On 29 December 1927 more eruptions took place and a new island emerged from the sea, Anak Krakatau – Child of Krakatoa – which is rumbling to this day, seemingly readying itself for another earth-shattering eruption.

Talk

Understanding the text

1 What is the article about?
2 The article reports three incidents. When and where does each take place?
3 In what way are the first and second incidents:
   a similar?   **b** different?

4 Why is the team of scientists going to the new island?
5 What caused the loss of life after the eruption of Krakatoa?

Looking at language

6 Explain these phrases in your own words.

a Richter scale	**b** imminent danger	**c** several months
d quietened down	**e** stripped away	**f** it has been estimated

7 Explain the meaning of these words as they are used in the article.
   Use a dictionary to help you.

a ejected	**b** eroded	**c** virtually
d submerged	**e** tsunami	**f** ensuing

Exploring the article

8 In addition to the text, how has the writer helped the reader to understand the article?
9 Give an example of a fact in the article.
10 Why do you think the writer gives exact dates and measurements in the article?
11 Why do you think that the number of people who died is only 'estimated'?
12 Make a list of questions you would like to ask about Krakatoa.

Taking it further

▶ (RB, Unit 7, Extension)

13 Plan an article on an imaginary island with a volcano that erupts.
    Make notes on:
    • facts you need to include.
    • opinions you would include.
    • how you would illustrate the article.
    • how you would lay out the article.

Talk

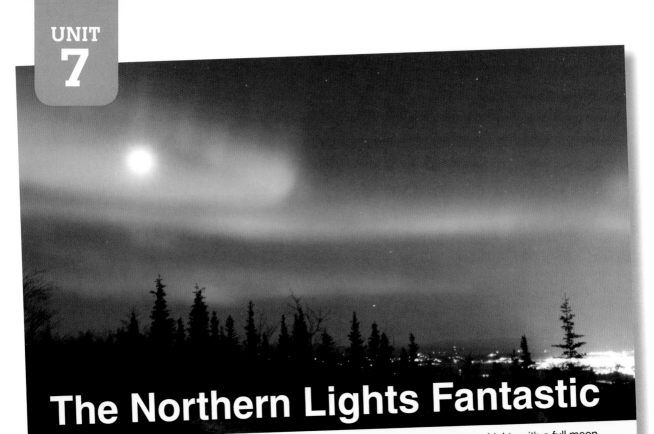

The Northern Lights Fantastic

A rare image of the Northern Lights with a full moon.

by Penny Stretton

The Northern Lights sweep startling colours across the frozen night sky as the moon rises over the snow.

A shock of yellow lights up the mountains in Yukon, Canada, threatening to outshine the full moon.

In the nearby Brooks Range, a glow of turquoise and pink bathe an igloo in unearthly light.

And waves of green dance around a streak of white and pink high above an Inuit monument, or inukshuk, in Hudson Bay, Manitoba.

Photographer Rolf Hicker has spent the last 10 years travelling thousands of miles with his wife Michelle to capture these amazing images.

The Aurora Borealis is only visible at night, and is best seen in winter. It is extremely difficult to capture the full glory of the Northern Lights, especially with a full moon – and most photographers don't

An Inuit inukshuk is illuminated by waves of green dancing lights.

bother. But Mr Hicker found a way. He said, 'It's the perfect time to show the Northern Lights with the landscape. If conditions are right, especially when it is very cold, you can experience one of the most amazing moments we ever have – a moonrise with the Aurora Borealis, all at the same time.'

He added: 'The reward for all the trouble is amazing – silence and dancing Northern Lights in the moonlight.'

Write

Understanding the text

1 Who wrote the article?

2 Name the three places the photographer has visited to photograph the Northern Lights.

3 What is the other name for the Northern Lights?

4 How many years have Mr Hicker and his wife been travelling to 'capture these amazing images'?

5 What are the best conditions to see the Northern Lights?

Looking at language

6 Explain the meaning of these words as they are used in the article. Use a dictionary to help you.

   a startling **b** threatening **c** outshine
   d bathe   **e** unearthly   **f** visible

Exploring the article

7 Why do you think the Northern Lights are 'best seen in winter'?

8 What impression do you get of Rolf Hicker?

9 Why do you think most photographers 'don't bother' to try to photograph the Northern Lights?

10 Would the article be interesting without the photographs? Why? Why not?

11 Explain how you think Rolf Hicker feels when he is watching the Northern Lights.

Taking it further

RB, Unit 7, Extension

12 Imagine you could interview Rolf Hicker about his travels and his photography. What questions would you ask him?

Write

Marley's Ghost

The cellar-door flew open with a booming sound, and then he heard the noise much louder, on the floors below; then coming up the stairs, then coming straight towards his door.

'It's humbug, still!' said Scrooge. 'I won't believe it.'

His colour changed though when, without a pause, it came on through the heavy door, and passed into the room before his eyes. Upon coming in, the dying flame leaped up, as though it cried, 'I know him! Marley's ghost!' and fell again.

The same face: the very same. Marley in his pigtail, usual waistcoat, tights, and boots … The chain he drew was clasped about his middle. It was long and wound about him like a tail. It was made of cash-boxes, keys, padlocks, ledgers, deeds and heavy purses wrought in steel. His body was transparent, so that Scrooge observing him, and looking through his waistcoat, could see the two buttons on his coat behind …

Nor did he believe it even now. Though he looked the phantom through and through and saw it standing before him. Though he felt the chilling influence of his death-cold eyes … he was still incredulous, and fought against his senses.

'How now!' said Scrooge, caustic and cold as ever. 'What do you want with me?'

'Much!' – Marley's voice, no doubt about it.

'Who are you?'

'Ask me who I *was*.'

'Who *were* you then?' said Scrooge, raising his voice …

'In life I was your partner, Jacob Marley … You don't believe in me,' observed the Ghost.

'I don't,' said Scrooge …

At this the spirit raised a frightful cry, and shook its chain with such a dismal and appalling noise, that Scrooge held on tight to his chair to save himself from falling in a swoon. But how much greater was his horror when, the phantom, taking off the bandage round his head as if it were too warm to wear indoors, its lower jaw dropped down upon its breast.

Scrooge fell upon his knees and clasped his hands before his face.

'Mercy!' he said. 'Dreadful apparition, why do you trouble me?'

'Man of the worldly mind!' replied the Ghost, 'do you believe in me or not?'

'I do,' said Scrooge. 'I must. But why do spirits walk the earth, and why do they come to me?'

'It is required of every man,' the Ghost returned, 'that the spirit within him should walk abroad among his fellow-men, and travel far and wide, and if that spirit goes not forth in life, it is condemned to do so after death. It is doomed to wander through the world – oh, woe is me – and witness what it cannot share, but might have shared on earth, and turned to happiness!' …

'But you were always a good man of business, Jacob,' faltered Scrooge …

'Business!' cried the Ghost, wringing his hands. 'Mankind was my business; the common welfare was my business; charity, mercy, forbearance … Hear me! My time is nearly gone.'

'I will,' said Scrooge, 'but don't be hard on me!' …

'I am here tonight to warn you, that you have yet a chance and hope of escaping my fate … You will be haunted by Three Spirits.'

'Is that the chance and hope you mentioned, Jacob?' Scrooge demanded in a faltering voice.

'It is.'

'I – I think I'd rather not,' said Scrooge.

'Without their visits,' said the Ghost, 'you cannot hope to shun the path I tread. Expect the first tomorrow, when the bell tolls one.'

A Christmas Carol, **Charles Dickens**

Understanding the text

1 What is the name of the ghost?

2 Who is he visiting?

3 Name two things the chain was made of.

4 How many spirits would Scrooge see?

5 What did the ghost tell Scrooge to expect tomorrow?

Looking at language

6 Explain the meaning of these words as they are used in the story.
Use a dictionary to help you.

a ledgers	**b** phantom	**c** incredulous	**d** caustic
e swoon	**f** apparition	**g** forbearance	**h** shun

Exploring the story

7 How does Scrooge feel about Marley:

a when he first appears?   **b** at the end of the extract?

8 Why do you think the ghost had to drag the chain around with him?

9 Marley spent all of his life thinking about 'business'. What should Marley
have thought more about when he was alive?

10 What warning was the ghost bringing to Scrooge?

11 In your own words, explain why you think Scrooge is being haunted.

Taking it further

▶ (RB, Unit 8, Extension)

12 Read again the conversation between Marley and Scrooge.
Rewrite it in modern English.

Teach

Hamlet, Prince of Denmark

The King has died suddenly and mysteriously. The Queen has married her dead husband's brother who has now become King. Prince Hamlet is very unhappy about his father's death and his mother's remarriage.

One bitterly cold winter night, on the wind-swept battlements of the royal castle at Elsinore the sentries were changing guard. Except for their shouts as they challenged each other and the muffled thunder of the sea on the rocks below, all was quiet; not a mouse was stirring.

Suddenly the sound of footsteps briskly marching …

'Halt! Who goes there?' cried Bernardo, the relief officer, as a figure rose up in front of him. He was so nervous that he had forgotten to wait to be challenged first.

'No, *you* answer *me*! Give me the password,' came the answer.

'"Long live the King."'

'Are you Bernardo?'

'Yes.'

'You're very punctual.'

'It's past midnight, Francisco. Get to bed. Horatio and Marcellus are sharing the watch with me. If you see them, tell them to hurry.'

'I can hear them coming – here they are,' said Francisco. And when he had challenged and greeted the two newcomers, he lowered his pike. Wishing them good night, he marched off down the rocky path to the barracks, relieved that his freezing watch was over and quite unaware that anything unusual had happened to disturb Bernardo.

'Has this ghost appeared again?' said Horatio, half jokingly.

'I have seen nothing,' said Bernardo.

'Horatio thinks we have only imagined it,' said Marcellus. 'He won't believe we have both seen it twice. That's why I have asked him to share our watch tonight in case it appears again.'

'Nonsense. I'm sure it won't appear,' said Horatio, who was too matter-of-fact and level-headed to be superstitious.

'Last night, at the stroke of one –' Bernardo began, then broke off abruptly.

A tall majestic figure had loomed out of the darkness and stood before them, shimmering in the moonlight. Armed from head to foot, the helmet visor raised, it had a pale and haggard face and grizzled beard and seemed to be floating in the air.

'It's like our dead King,' Bernardo gasped.

'Exactly like him,' agreed Horatio, harrowed with fear and wonder.

He steadied his nerves and strode boldly forward. Holding his sword in front of him hilt upwards like a cross, he tried to question it. But it stalked away into the shadows as if it had been offended.

What could this vision mean? Clad in the same armour he had worn in the Norwegian war, it was the very image of the dead King. Why had he returned to haunt them? Could it be because the Norwegians, defeated in the recent war, were threatening to attack again and recover the land they had lost? As they paced up and down, Horatio and the two officers anxiously discussed these questions but could find no answer.

Suddenly, when the night was almost over, the ghost appeared again. Horatio stood in its path and challenged it. It seemed about to speak some message, when in the distance a cock crowed. Then it turned its head and began to drift away.

They cried out; they tried to trap it, to strike it with their pikes, but it melted into the shadows and all they struck was empty air.

Already the first gleams of dawn had splashed the eastern hills. Their watch over, the three soldiers left the battlements and returned to the palace, determined to tell Hamlet what they had seen. Hamlet was the dead King's son. Perhaps the ghost, who had been dumb to them, would speak to him.

The Enchanted Island, **Ian Serraillier**

Talk

Understanding the text

1 What is the setting for the extract?
2 Who are the characters?
3 What unusual thing have the two soldiers seen?
4 What happened when Horatio 'tried to question it'?
5 When they left the battlements, what were the three soldiers going to do?

Looking at language

6 Explain these phrases in your own words.

    a wind-swept   **b** not a mouse was stirring   **c** imagined it
    d level-headed   **e** challenged it   **f** melted into the shadows

7 Explain the meaning of these words as they are used in the story.
Use a dictionary to help you.

    a battlements   **b** punctual   **c** pike
    d superstitious   **e** majestic   **f** haggard
    g harrowed   **h** offended

Exploring the story

 8 Why do you think the ghostly scene is set 'one bitterly cold winter night'?
 9 What impression do you get of Horatio?
10 Why do you think the ghost 'began to drift away' when the 'cock crowed'?
11 Why do the soldiers think the ghost might talk to Hamlet?

Taking it further

▶ (RB, Unit 8, Extension)

12 Make the extract into a playscript and prepare it for performance.
You will need:
- the scene
- the characters
- the dialogue
- stage directions

Talk

The Ghostly Girl

Mandy awoke suddenly in the night, trembling with fear. Moonlight flooded her bedroom with silver and shadow. It was only a dream, she told herself, only a dream. So why was she shivering in a warm bed?

A memory of the dream returned and she threw back the bedclothes and switched on the light. It had all seemed so real, and she'd never had a fright like that before.

She wrapped a dressing-gown around her and opened the door. The house was quiet, the passage in darkness, as she felt her way along the wall to her brother's room. She opened the door and closed it behind her, switched on the light.

Joe's room was full of aeroplane models, and she had to move carefully to avoid them. She sat on the edge of his bed and shook him hard; Joe was a heavy sleeper.

Presently, her brother stirred. 'What's up, then? Mandy …'

'I had a nightmare, Joe. It scared me – I've got to talk to somebody.'

Joe was twelve, two years younger than his sister, and sturdy, with unruly fair hair.

Mandy shuddered. 'It was horrid!'

Joe sat up reluctantly; he was still sleepy. 'What was it about?'

'I was walking along, through a mist, and all round me were ruins. It was nowhere I've ever seen, I'm sure of that. And then *she* came towards me, through the mist. Her feet didn't touch the ground – she just drifted along. I could see right through her, Joe. She was a ghost, a girl of about my age in a long dress, and with a pale face. Her mouth was moving as if she was trying to say something, but I couldn't hear what it was – like watching the old silent movies on telly. That's all, really, because I woke up. But it was so real.' She forced a laugh. 'I don't know why I was scared so much – it was only a dream.'

Joe rubbed sleep from his eyes and looked hard at his sister. 'You do look a bit white … Still, I never heard of anyone dreaming a ghost before.' He sounded impressed.

Mandy stood up. 'I'll be all right now, Joe. Thanks for listening.'

She tiptoed back to her room, and it was a long time before she fell asleep.

A week later, Mandy dreamed again. She stood among the ruins of an old house and it was dark. The ghost girl appeared before her, rippling as if seen through water. She felt icy cold. The ghost drifted nearer and lifted an arm, reaching out a hand to touch her …

Mandy awoke abruptly, soaked with sweat, her heart thumping wildly. She pushed bedclothes into her mouth to stop herself screaming. It was ridiculous, she thought, scared silly by a dream …

At the breakfast table, her mother commented, 'You look off-colour, Mandy. Are you sleeping all right?'

Joe hastily swallowed a spoonful of cereal. 'Was it the dream again?'

Their father looked up from his newspaper crossword. 'What dream's this? First I've heard of it.'

'She dreamed a ghost,' Joe said proudly.

Write

Dream Ghost, **Sydney J Bounds**

Understanding the text

1 Why was Mandy 'shivering'?

2 Who did she go to talk to?

3 What did the girl in the dream look like?

4 When did Mandy have the dream again?

5 At what point did Mandy wake up:
   a in the first dream?
   b in the second dream?

Looking at language

6 Explain these phrases in your own words.

   a heavy sleeper   b silent movies   c looked hard at   d off-colour

7 Explain the meaning of these words as they are used in the story.
   Use a dictionary to help you.

   a avoid   b stirred   c nightmare
   d unruly   e reluctantly   f ridiculous

Exploring the story

8 Find evidence in the story to show how Mandy reacted to:
   a the first dream.   b the second dream.

9 Do you think Mandy was more or less frightened by the second dream?
   Explain your reasons.

10 Why do you think Mandy told her brother about the dream but not her parents?

11 What impression do you get of Mandy?

12 What impression do you get of Joe?

13 How do you think Mandy's parents will react, now they know about the dream?

Taking it further

▶ (RB, Unit 8, Extension)

14 Read the three extracts about ghosts again.
   Which one do you think is the most enjoyable? Explain your reasons.

Write

UNIT 9

The Brook

I come from haunts of coot and hern,
   I make a sudden sally,
And sparkle out among the fern,
   To bicker down a valley.

By thirty hills I hurry down,
   Or slip between the ridges,
By twenty thorps, a little town,
   And half a hundred bridges.

I chatter over stony ways,
   In little sharps and trebles,
I bubble into eddying bays,
   I babble on the pebbles.

With many a curve my banks I fret
   By many a field and fallow,
Any many a fairy foreland set
   With willow-weed and mallow.

I chatter, chatter, as I flow
   To join the brimming river,
For men may come and men may go,
   But I go on for ever.

I wind about, and in and out,
   With here a blossom sailing,
And here and there a lusty trout,
   And here and there a grayling.

And here and there a foamy flake
   Upon me, as I travel
With many a silvery waterbreak
   Above the golden gravel,

And draw them all along, and flow
   To join the brimming river,
For men may come and men may go,
   But I go on for ever.

I slip, I slide, I gloom, I glance,
   Among my skimming swallows;
I make the netted sunbeam dance
   Against my sandy shallows.

I murmur under moon and stars
   In brambly wildernesses;
I linger by my shingly bars;
   I loiter round my cresses;

And out again I curve and flow
   To join the brimming river,
For men may come and men may go,
   But I go on for ever.

Alfred Lord Tennyson

Teach

Understanding the text

1 Where does the brook come from?

2 Where is it going?

3 When is the brook moving quickly?

4 When is the brook moving slowly?

5 How long does the brook go on for?

Looking at language

6 Explain the meaning of these words as they are used in the poem. Use a dictionary to help you.

a haunts   b sally   c thorps

d fret   e foreland   f loiter

7 Can you find in the poem:

a three types of birds?   b two types of fish?   c three type of plants?

Exploring the poem

8 What things does the brook do, that we would normally think of humans doing?

9 If the brook was human, what sort of person do you think it would be?

10 Why do you think the poet has used the words 'chatter', 'babble' and 'murmur'?

11 How do you know the brook goes on during the night as well as during the day?

12 Explain in your own words the meaning of the last two lines of the poem.

13 Explain why you like or do not like the poem.

Taking it further

▶ RB, Unit 9, Extension

14 In groups, learn and recite the poem. Use different people to say different verses.

Teach

The River's Story

I remember when life was good.
I shilly-shallied across meadows,
Tumbled down mountains,
I laughed and gurgled through woods,
Stretched and yawned in a myriad
    of floods.
Insects, weightless as sunbeams,
Settled upon my skin to drink.
I wore lily-pads like medals.
Fish, lazy and battle-scarred,
Gossiped beneath them.
The damselflies were my ballerinas,
The pike my ambassadors.
Kingfishers, disguised as rainbows,
Were my secret agents.
It was a sweet-time, a gone-time,
A time before factories grew,
Brick by greedy brick,
And left me cowering
In monstrous shadows.
Like drunken giants

They vomited their poison into me.
Tonight a scattering of vagrant bluebells,
Dwarfed by the same poisons,
Toll my ending.
Children, come and find me if you wish,
I am your inheritance.
Behind the derelict housing-estates
You will discover my remnants.
Clogged with garbage and junk
To an open sewer I've shrunk,
I, who have flowed through history,
Who have seen hamlets become villages,
Villages become towns, towns become cit
Am reduced to a trickle of filth
Beneath the still, burning stars.

Brian Patten

Talk

Understanding the text

1 Where did the river flow 'when life was good'?

2 Name three groups of living things associated with the river.

3 What has happened around the river that has changed everything?

4 What do the factories put into the river?

5 What is now left of the river?

Looking at language

6 Explain these phrases in your own words.

a shilly-shallied   b battle-scarred   c a gone-time
d toll my ending   e your inheritance   f reduced to

7 Explain the meaning of these words as they are used in the poem.
   Use a dictionary to help you.

a myriad   b ambassadors   c cowering   d vomited
e vagrant   f derelict   g remnants   h trickle

Exploring the poem

8 Why do you think the poet has made the river appear human?

9 If the river was human, how do you think it felt when:

a 'life was good'?   b 'factories grew'?

10 Why do you think the fish were 'battle-scarred'?

11 Why do you think the factories are described as 'greedy'?

12 What does the river mean when it says it has 'flowed through history'?

13 What do you think the poem is warning us about?

Taking it further

▶ (RB, Unit 9, Extension)

14 Using the information in the poem, make a poster to warn people
    about polluting rivers. Write the text as if it were the river speaking.

Talk

Coral Reef

I am a teeming city;
An underwater garden
Where fishes fly;
A lost forest
of skeleton trees;
A home for starry anemones;
A hiding place for frightened fishes;
A skulking place for prowling predators;
An alien world
Whose unseen monsters
Watch with luminous eyes;
An ancient palace topped by
Improbable towers;
A mermaid's maze;
A living barrier built on
Uncountable small deaths;
An endlessly growing sculpture;
A brittle mystery;
A vanishing trick;
A dazzling wonder
More magical than all
Your earthbound dreams;
I am a priceless treasure;
A precious heirloom,
And I am yours

To love
Or to lose
As you choose.

Clare Bevan

Write

Understanding the text

1 Find three things in the poem which are normally found on land.

2 For what do 'frightened fishes' use the coral reef?

3 What phrase in the poem tells you the coral reef is always getting bigger?

4 What word tells you that the coral reef is very fragile and can break easily?

5 What choice do people have to make about coral reefs?

Looking at language

6 Find adjectives in the poem that describe:

> **a** garden   **b** forest   **c** predators
>
> **d** palace   **e** treasure   **f** heirloom

7 Explain the meaning of these words as they are used in the poem. Use a dictionary to help you.

> **a** teeming   **b** skeleton   **c** skulking
>
> **d** luminous   **e** brittle   **f** heirloom

Exploring the poem

8 Explain what the poet means when she says that the coral reef is 'built on / Uncountable small deaths'.

9 What do you think the 'unseen monsters' are?

10 Why do you think the towers are described as 'improbable'?

11 The poet has given the coral reef a voice. What warning is the coral reef giving to the reader?

12 If the coral reef were human, what sort of person do you think it would be?

13 Using what you have learnt from the poem, write briefly about why you think we should, or should not, protect coral reefs.

Taking it further

▶ (RB, Unit 9, Extension)

14 Read the three poems again. Choose which one you like the best and explain your reasons.

(Write)

Endurance's Last Voyage

In 1914, Ernest Shackleton set off to cross Antarctica via the South Pole. By 1915, his ship Endurance *was trapped in ice. The ship was being crushed. Shackleton and his fellow explorers had to abandon the ship before it sank.*

This morning, our last on the ship, the weather was clear, with a gentle south-south-easterly to south-south-westerly breeze. From the crow's nest there was no sign of land of any sort. The pressure was increasing steadily, and the passing hours brought no relief or respite for the ship.

The attack of the ice reached its climax at 4pm. The ship was hove stern up by the pressure, and the driving floe, moving laterally across the stern, split the rudder and tore out the rudder-post and stern-post. Then, while we watched, the ice loosened and the *Endurance* sank a little. The decks were breaking upwards and the water was pouring in below. Again the pressure began, and at 5pm, I ordered all hands on to the ice.

The twisting, grinding floes were working their will at last on the ship. It was a sickening sensation to feel the decks breaking up under one's feet, the great beams bending and then snapping with a noise like heavy gun-fire …

Just before leaving, I looked down the engine-room skylight as I stood on the quivering deck, and saw the engines dropping sideways as the stays and bed-plates gave way. I cannot describe the impression of relentless destruction that was forced upon me as I looked down and around. The floes, with the force of millions of tons of moving ice behind them, were simply annihilating the ship …

South, **Sir Ernest Shackleton**

Understanding the text

1 Who is the author of the autobiography?

2 What is the name of the ship?

3 What was the weather like on the last morning on the ship?

4 What happened at 4pm?

5 At what time did they leave the ship and go on to the ice?

Looking at language

6 Explain these phrases in your own words.

> **a** increasing steadily   **b** all hands   **c** relentless destruction

7 Explain the meaning of these words as they are used in the autobiography. Use a dictionary to help you.

> **a** respite   **b** climax   **c** floe   **d** laterally   **e** annihilating

Exploring the autobiography

8 Find evidence in the extract that shows Shackleton was very upset about losing the ship.

9 Find two words or phrases that show Shackleton writes about the ice as if it were human.

10 Find an example where Shackleton:

   a records a fact.   **b** expresses an opinion.

11 What impression do you get of Shackleton?

Taking it further

RB, Unit 10, Extension

12 Do you think the extract gives a good impression of the awful situation Shackleton and his men find themselves in or not? Explain your reasons.

Teach

20 HRS, 40 MIN ...
Our Flight in the *Friendship*

In 1928, Amelia Earhart was the first woman to cross the Atlantic by aeroplane.
Along with Wilmer (Bill) Stultz and Louis ('Slim') Gordon, she flew from Trepassey in Canada
to Burry Port in the United Kingdom.

> Can't use radio at all. Coming down now in a rather
> clear spot. 2,500ft. Everything sliding forward.
> 8:50. 2 Boats!!!!
> Trans steamer.
> Try to get bearing. Radio won't work. One hr's gas. Mess.
> All craft cutting our course. Why?

So the log ends.

Its last page records that we had but one hour's supply of gas left; that the time for reaching Ireland had passed; that the course of the vessel sighted perplexed us; that our radio was useless.

Where were we? Should we keep faith with our course and continue?

'Mess' epitomised the blackness of the moment. Were we beaten?

We all favoured sticking to the course. We had to. With faith lost in that, it was hopeless to carry on. Besides, when last we checked it, before the radio went dead, the plane had been holding true.

We circled the *America*, although having no idea of her identity at the time. With the radio crippled, in an effort to get our position, Bill scribbled a note. The note and an orange to weight it, I tied in a bag with an absurd piece of silver cord. As we circled the *America*, the bag was dropped through the hatch. But the combination of our speed, the movement of the vessel, the wind and the lightness of the missile was too much for our marksmanship. We tried another shot, using our remaining orange. No luck.

Should we seek safety and try to come down beside the steamer? Perhaps one reason the attempt was never attempted was the roughness of the sea which not only made a landing difficult but a take-off impossible.

Bill leaped to the radio with the hope of at least receiving a message. At some moment in the excitement, before I closed the hatch which opens in the bottom of the fuselage I lay flat and took a photograph. This, I am told, is the first one made of a vessel at sea from a plane in trans-Atlantic flight ...

We could see only a few miles of water, which melted into the greyness on all sides. The ceiling was so low we could fly at an altitude of only 500 feet. As we moved, our miniature world of visibility, bounded by its walls of mist, moved with us. Half an hour later into it suddenly swam a fishing vessel. In a matter of minutes a fleet of small craft, probably fishing vessels, were almost below us. Happily their course paralleled ours. Although the gasoline in the tanks was vanishing fast, we began to feel land – some land – must be near. It might not be Ireland, but any land would do just then.

Bill, of course, was at the controls. Slim, gnawing a sandwich, sat beside him, when out of the mists there grew a blue shadow, in appearance no more solid than hundreds of other nebulous 'landscapes' we had sighted before. For a while Slim studied it, then turned and called Bill's attention to it.

It was land!

Amelia Earhart

Talk

Understanding the text

1 From where did the flight take off?

2 What was the:
   a intended destination?   **b** the actual destination?

3 What was the name of the aeroplane?

4 How long did the flight take?

5 What were the two main problems towards the end of the flight?

Looking at language

6 Explain these phrases in your own words.

> **a** keep faith   **b** holding true   **c** I am told

7 Explain the meaning of these words as they are used in the autobiography.
   Use a dictionary to help you.

> **a** bearing   **b** log   **c** identity   **d** perplexed
> **e** epitomised   **f** fuselage   **g** altitude   **h** nebulous

Exploring the autobiography

8 What do you think the *America* was?

9 When Bill dropped the notes, what was he trying to find out?

10 There are four reasons in the text why they had 'no luck' with the notes.
   Find two reasons.

11 Reread the paragraph beginning 'We could see only a few miles of water …'
   How do you think they were feeling:
   a before they saw the fishing vessel?   **b** after they saw the fishing vessel?

12 What impression do you get of Amelia Earhart?

13 Would you have liked to be in the plane with Earhart on that journey or not?
   Explain your reasons.

Taking it further

▶ RB, Unit 10, Extension

14 The flight across the Atlantic Ocean is 2,246 miles. Look at the
   photograph of Amelia Earhart and her plane.
   Why do you think she went on such a dangerous journey?

Talk

UNIT 10

Touching the Void

In June 1985, Joe Simpson and Simon Yates climbed 6,344m to the top of Siula Grande in the Andes. On the way down, disaster struck! Joe's ice hammer came out of the mountain wall and …

… there was a sharp cracking sound and my right hand, gripping the axe, pulled down. The sudden jerk turned me outwards and instantly I was falling.

I hit the slope at the base of the cliff before I saw it coming. I was facing into the slope and both knees locked as I struck it. I felt a shattering blow in my knee, felt bones splitting, and screamed. The impact catapulted me over backwards and down the slope of the East Face. I slid, head-first, on my back. The rushing speed of it confused me. I thought of the drop below but felt nothing. Simon would be ripped off the mountain. He couldn't hold this. I screamed again as I jerked to a sudden violent stop …

Everything was still, silent. My thoughts raced madly. Then pain flooded down my thigh – a fierce burning fire coming down the inside of my thigh, seeming to ball in my groin, building and building until I cried out at it, and my breathing came in ragged gasps. My leg! … My leg!

I hung, head down, on my back, left leg tangled in the rope above me, and my right leg hanging slackly to one side. I lifted my head from the snow and stared, up across my chest, at a grotesque distortion in the right knee, twisting the leg into a strange zigzag. I didn't connect it with the pain which burnt in my groin. That had nothing to do with my knee. I kicked my left leg free of the rope and swung round until I was hanging against the snow on my chest, feet down. The pain eased. I kicked my left foot into the slope and stood up.

A wave of nausea surged over me. I pressed my face into the snow, and the sharp cold seemed to calm me. Something terrible, something dark with dread occurred to me, and as I thought about it I felt the dark thought break into panic: 'I've broken my leg, that's it. I'm dead. Everyone said it … if there's just two of you a broken ankle could turn into a death sentence … if it's broken … if … It doesn't hurt so much, maybe I've just ripped something.'

I kicked my right leg against the slope, feeling sure it wasn't broken. My knee exploded. Bone grated, and the fireball rushed from groin to knee. I screamed. I looked down at the knee and could see it was broken, yet I tried not to believe what I was seeing. It wasn't just broken, it was ruptured, twisted, crushed, and I could see the kink in the joint and knew what had happened. The impact had driven my lower leg up through the knee joint.

Joe Simpson

Write

Understanding the text

1 Name the two men climbing in the Andes.

2 Which mountain were they climbing?

3 How high is the mountain?

4 What side of the mountain were they on?

5 What could a minor injury, such as a broken ankle, mean for only two climbers on the mountain?

Looking at language

6 Explain these phrases in your own words.

a grotesque distortion   **b** wave of nausea   **c** surged over

7 Explain the meaning of these words as they are used in the autobiography. Use a dictionary to help you.

a locked   **b** catapulted   **c** ripped
d slackly   **e** ruptured   **f** impact

Exploring the autobiography

8 What do you think Joe meant when he wrote 'Simon would be ripped off the mountain. He couldn't hold this'?

9 Explain, in your own words, what was the 'something dark with dread' that occurred to Joe.

10 Joe's right leg was injured. Why do you think he kicked it 'against the slope'?

11 What impression do you get of Joe Simpson?

Taking it further

▶ (RB, Unit 10, Extension)

12 Simon was above Joe on the mountain. He couldn't see what happened but he knew something was wrong.
Imagine you are Simon and write briefly about the incident from your point of view. Remember that as well as facts, you need to include your thoughts and feelings.

Write

How to Use This Book

This heading tells you the name of the text.

The red questions are about understanding what's happened in the text.

This heading tells you about the unit topic.

The purple questions are about words and phrases used in the text.

UNIT
8

Exploring Atmosphere and Tension

Marley's Ghost

The cellar-door flew open with a booming sound, and then he heard the noise much louder, on the floors below; then coming up the stairs, then coming straight towards his door.

'It's humbug, still!' said Scrooge. 'I won't believe it.'

His colour changed though when, without a pause, it came on through the heavy door, and passed into the room before his eyes. Upon coming in, the dying flame leaped up, as though it cried, 'I know him! Marley's ghost!' and fell again.

The same face: the very same. Marley in his pigtail, usual waistcoat, tights, and boots … The chain he drew was clasped about his middle. It was long and wound about him like a tail. It was made of cash-boxes, keys, padlocks, ledgers, deeds and heavy purses wrought in steel. His body was transparent, so that Scrooge observing him, and looking through his waistcoat, could see the two buttons on his coat behind …

Nor did he believe it even now. Though he looked the phantom through and through and saw it standing before him. Though he felt the chilling influence of his death-cold eyes … he was still incredulous, and fought against his senses.

'How now!' said Scrooge, caustic and cold as ever. 'What do you want with me?'

'Much!' – Marley's voice, no doubt about it.

'Who are you?'

'Ask me who I was.'

'Who were you then?' said Scrooge, raising his voice …

'In life I was your partner, Jacob Marley … You don't believe in me,' observed the Ghost.

'I don't,' said Scrooge …

At this the spirit raised a frightful cry, and shook its chain with such a dismal and appalling noise, that Scrooge held on tight to his chair to save himself from falling in a swoon. But how

much greater was his horror when, the phantom, taking off the bandage round his head as if it were too warm to wear indoors, its lower jaw dropped down upon its breast.

Scrooge fell upon his knees and clasped his hands before his face.

'Mercy!' he said. 'Dreadful apparition, why do you trouble me?'

'Man of the worldly mind!' replied the Ghost, 'do you believe in me or not?'

'I do,' said Scrooge. 'I must. But why do spirits walk the earth, and why do they come to me?'

'It is required of every man,' the Ghost returned, 'that the spirit within him should walk abroad among his fellow-men, and travel far and wide, and if that spirit goes not forth in life, it is condemned to do so after death. It is doomed to wander through the world – oh, woe is me – and witness what it cannot share, but might have shared on earth, and turned to happiness!' …

'But you were always a good man of business, Jacob,' faltered Scrooge …

'Business!' cried the Ghost, wringing his hands. 'Mankind was my business; the common welfare was my business; charity, mercy, forbearance … Hear me! My time is nearly gone.'

'I will,' said Scrooge, 'but don't be hard on me!' …

'I am here tonight to warn you, that you have yet a chance and hope of escaping my fate … You will be haunted by Three Spirits.'

'Is that the chance and hope you mentioned, Jacob?' Scrooge demanded in a faltering voice.

'It is.'

'I – I think I'd rather not,' said Scrooge.

'Without their visits,' said the Ghost, 'you cannot hope to shun the path I tread. Expect the first tomorrow, when the bell tolls one.'

A Christmas Carol, **Charles Dickens**

Teach

46

Understanding the text

1 What is the name of the ghost?

2 Who is he visiting?

3 Name two things the chain was made of.

4 How many spirits would Scrooge see?

5 What did the ghost tell Scrooge to expect tomorrow?

Looking at language

6 Explain the meaning of these words as they are used in the story. Use a dictionary to help you.

a ledgers	**b** phantom	**c** incredulous	**d** caustic
e swoon	**f** apparition	**g** forbearance	**h** shun

Exploring the story

7 How does Scrooge feel about Marley:

   a when he first appears?   **b** at the end of the extract?

8 Why do you think the ghost had to drag the chain around with him?

9 Marley spent all of his life thinking about 'business'. What should Marley have thought more about when he was alive?

10 What warning was the ghost bringing to Scrooge?

11 In your own words, explain why you think Scrooge is being haunted.

Taking it further

▶ RB, Unit 8, Extension

12 Read again the conversation between Marley and Scrooge. Rewrite it in modern English.

Teach

47

The author's name is here.

The green questions are about the unit topic, and may ask you to read between the lines—to work out things that the author implies but does not state.

The blue questions ask you to think more deeply about the text.

This tells you that there's an Extension resource sheet relating to this question in the Resources & Assessment Book.